IS THERE REALLY SOMEBODY FOR EVERYBODY?

DATING, COMPANIONSHIP, AND THE REALITY OF RELATIONSHIPS IN THE LATER YEARS

ALICE TRUMAN

TOP ARTISTS 4U LLC

First Printing, 2026

ISBN

Paperback - 13: 978-1-968871-85-7

Ebook - 13: 978-1-968871-86-4

Top Artists 4 U LLC

15021 Ventura Blvd. #783 Sherman Oaks, CA 91403

TopArtists4U@gmail.com

CONTENTS

INTRODUCTION

THE QUESTION WE ALL GREW UP BELIEVING

Most of us grew up hearing the same comforting idea: there's somebody out there for everybody. It's one of those sayings people repeat so often that we rarely stop to question it. When we were younger, it sounded hopeful - almost like a promise life would eventually deliver. Somewhere out there, we were told, was a person meant for us. Someone we would meet, fall in love with, build a life with, and grow old beside.

When we are in our twenties or thirties, that idea feels natural. Life is still unfolding. People are building careers, building families, and building futures. Relationships often grow out of that momentum. Two people meet, fall in love, and begin constructing something together, piece by piece, step by step.

But something shifts as we move into the later seasons of life. People start looking around and quietly wondering if that old saying is really as simple as it once sounded. By the time someone reaches their fifties, sixties, or beyond, life has already happened. There have been marriages, divorces, losses, career changes, children, grandchildren, financial successes, financial struggles, health scares, and all the other twists and turns that come with living long enough to accumulate a real story. And all of those experiences change the relationship landscape in ways many people never anticipated when they were younger.

A lot of people find themselves single again at a stage of life where they never imagined they would be. Some are divorced after decades of marriage. Some have lost a spouse they believed they would grow old with. Others drifted apart from someone they once thought would always be there. There are also people who spent years focused on work, raising children, or caring for family members, and one day found themselves in a quiet house wondering what comes next.

At this point in life, the question of relationships begins to mean something different. It's no longer just about romance or passion. For many people, it becomes about something deeper and more practical - companionship. Someone to talk to. Someone to share ordinary days with. Someone who notices if you're not feeling well or checks in just to make sure you're okay. Someone who understands the stage of life you're in because they're walking through it too.

That kind of companionship can matter more than people sometimes want to admit. Many people say they enjoy their independence, and often that's true. But getting older alone can feel different than people imagined when they were younger, and the quiet underneath that independence isn't always as comfortable as it looks from the outside.

This book is not about fairy tales or romantic fantasies. It's not about pretending that relationships later in life are simple or easy, and it certainly isn't about offering some magical formula for finding the perfect partner. Instead, it's about having an honest conversation about something millions of people are living through but rarely talk about openly: dating later in life, searching for companionship, and figuring out whether it is still possible to build a meaningful connection when life is already well underway.

The truth is that relationships in the later years come with realities that didn't exist when we were younger. People are not simply individuals anymore - they come with entire life structures. Adult children and grandchildren. Ex-spouses still connected through family events or shared history. Financial histories, retirement plans, and property they've spent years building. In younger years, two people usually construct a life together from the ground up. Later in life, two people are trying to merge lives that have already been built, and that is a completely different challenge.

There are also the things people often think about but rarely say directly. Questions about money. Questions about health. Questions about whether someone is looking for a partner or looking for someone to take care of them. These are real concerns, even if they feel uncomfortable to voice. And there is another reality worth naming honestly: many people say they want companionship, but the list of requirements they carry can quietly eliminate most of the people who might actually be available to them. Someone must be financially stable, must own a home, must be healthy, must be attractive, must arrive without too much baggage, and must fit seamlessly into an already established life.

Stack those conditions together and the field of potential partners becomes very small - while the search continues and the right person never seems to appear.

This book is not here to judge anyone for those concerns. Many of them are understandable. Life teaches people to be cautious, and past disappointments can make anyone protective of their independence and emotional safety. But if we are going to talk honestly about companionship later in life, we have to be willing to look at the full picture. That means talking about loneliness, expectations, fear, and the practical realities that come with aging. It means looking clearly at what people are truly searching for at this stage - and whether how they're searching is actually helping them find it.

The truth is that many people are not chasing the kind of passionate love they pursued when they were younger. What they are searching for is something quieter and steadier - someone they genuinely enjoy being around, someone who makes the later years feel less lonely, someone who can share the everyday moments that still make life worth living.

This book is simply an invitation to have that conversation honestly. Not as a lecture, and not as a set of rules, but as a real and human discussion about relationships, companionship, and the complicated question that many people eventually find themselves asking: Is there really somebody for everybody?

1

THE LONELINESS NOBODY TALKS ABOUT

Robert had a full life, by any reasonable measure. Two adult children who called regularly. A neighbor he had coffee with on Saturday mornings. A retirement that gave him the freedom to do whatever he wanted with his days. And yet, most evenings, he sat in a house that felt larger than it used to and watched the hours pass in a quiet that had gradually stopped feeling peaceful. He wasn't miserable. He wasn't falling apart. He simply missed having someone there - not for any dramatic reason, but for the small, ordinary ones. Someone to say goodnight to. Someone who would notice, without being told, that he seemed a little off today.

He never mentioned any of this to his children. He didn't want them to worry.

Loneliness is one of those things people don't like to admit out loud. Saying the word can make a person feel weak, needy, or somehow unsuccessful at life. So most people keep it to themselves. They go about their days, see friends occasionally, talk to family members, and from the outside everything looks fine. But when the day is over and the house gets quiet, many people are sitting in that silence more than they would ever admit.

For most people, loneliness doesn't arrive suddenly. It creeps in slowly as life shifts around them. Children grow up and move away. Friends get busy with their own worlds. Marriages end through divorce or loss. Work that once filled entire days eventually slows down or stops altogether. One day a person looks around and realizes the rhythm of their life has changed, and the number of people they interact with regularly is smaller than it used to be.

This is especially true as people move through their later years. Society talks constantly about youth, productivity, and ambition, but it rarely talks honestly about what happens emotionally as people age. A person can be financially comfortable, physically active, and still carry a quiet sense of isolation - not because they are incapable of being alone, but because human beings were simply never designed to experience life entirely by themselves.

Companionship matters more than many people want to admit. It isn't always about romance. Sometimes it's about something much simpler: having someone present. Someone to share a conversation with over dinner. Someone to call when something funny happens during the day. Someone who knows the small details of your life without needing a long explanation. Those ordinary interactions can seem unremarkable from the outside, but they create a sense of connection that becomes conspicuous the moment it's gone.

One of the more surprising things about loneliness is that it rarely looks the way people imagine. Most people assume it means having no one at all. But a person can have children, grandchildren, and a circle of friends and still feel lonely in a specific, particular way. Family relationships are deeply meaningful, but they don't always fill the same space that a companion fills. Children have their own lives and responsibilities. Friends have their own routines. Family gatherings happen occasionally, but everyday life still moves forward one quiet day at a time.

That's where companionship takes on a different meaning as people grow older. In earlier years, relationships are often driven by attraction, excitement, and the shared work of building a future. Later in life, the desire for companionship tends to come from somewhere more practical and more human. People begin thinking about who they share their time with. Who notices when they're present. And who would notice if they weren't.

Another thing that makes loneliness difficult to talk about is pride. Many people have built independent lives - worked hard, raised families, handled whatever came at them. Admitting they would like someone beside them can feel like admitting defeat. So instead of saying what they actually mean, people say things like, "I'm fine on my own," or "I don't really need anyone." And sometimes that's partially true. Independence can be genuinely good. But independence and companionship are not opposites, and choosing one doesn't have to mean giving up the other.

There is also a broader cultural shift that makes this conversation more important than ever. More people are living alone than at any previous point in modern history. Divorce among older adults has increased significantly - a trend researchers now call "gray divorce." And because people are living longer, someone who finds themselves single in their late fifties may still have two or three full decades of life ahead. That is a long time to spend entirely alone, if companionship is something they genuinely want.

Technology has changed the way people try to address this. Online dating platforms have become common among people over fifty, and for some they genuinely open doors that wouldn't otherwise exist. For others, the experience introduces a new set of frustrations. But regardless of how people meet, the reason so many of them are looking in the first place tends to be the same: they don't want to go through the rest of their lives alone.

What makes this stage of life complicated is that people are no longer starting from the same place they once were. When someone was dating in their twenties or thirties, there were fewer responsibilities, fewer emotional scars, and a natural flexibility that came with a life still being shaped. Later in life, people arrive carrying full histories. Some of those experiences have made them wiser. Some have made them cautious. And some have made them quietly hesitant to try again - even when the desire for connection hasn't gone anywhere.

That hesitation is understandable. When someone has been through divorce, betrayal, or the particular grief of losing a spouse, the idea of opening their life to another person can feel genuinely risky. The want is there. It simply has to compete with the fear of repeating something painful.

Still, the need for connection remains. Even people who have built a real comfort with solitude often notice that certain moments feel different when experienced alone. Celebrations are quieter. Difficult days are heavier. An achievement can feel strangely hollow when there's no one nearby to share it with.

None of this means every person requires a romantic partner to live a meaningful life. Many people do live richly, surrounded by family and community and friendship. But it does mean that the desire for companionship is not a weakness or a failure. It is a natural and deeply human feeling - and for many people, it is the quiet force that eventually brings them back to the question of whether there might still be room in their life for someone new.

That question - sometimes hopeful, sometimes frustrating, sometimes just persistent - is where this book begins.

2

WHY SO MANY OLDER ADULTS ARE SINGLE

If you had asked most people in their twenties what life would look like when they reached their late fifties or sixties, many of them would have given a similar answer. Still married. Kids grown and out of the house. Maybe thinking about retirement, maybe traveling more. But in most of those imagined futures, there was still someone sitting across the table at dinner.

Life, however, does not follow the scripts people write for it when they are young.

One of the most straightforward reasons so many people find themselves single later in life is that relationships which once seemed permanent eventually changed. Some marriages ended in divorce after many years together. Others ended because a spouse passed away. And in some cases, two people simply grew apart over time, not through any single dramatic event but through the slow drift that can happen when two lives gradually move in different directions.

Divorce among people over fifty has become far more common than it was a generation ago. Researchers have given it a name - gray divorce

- and the numbers behind it tell an interesting story. Couples who spent decades together sometimes reach a point where the life they built no longer fits who they have each become. In many cases, the marriage held together through the shared work of raising children, and when that chapter ends, the couple looks at each other across a quieter house and realizes the foundation beneath them has shifted. Other times the reasons go deeper: long-unresolved conflict, emotional distance that accumulated gradually, or simply the recognition that the person they are today is not the same person who made those early promises.

Then there are people who lose a spouse after many years together. This is a different kind of experience entirely — not the ending of something that stopped working, but the sudden absence of something that was still very much alive. Grief reshapes daily life in ways that are difficult to fully describe until you've lived them. Routines that once felt automatic become reminders. The idea of building a new connection can seem almost inconceivable at first, and for some people it remains that way for a long time. For others, the loneliness that eventually settles in becomes something they want to address, even if they're not sure how to begin.

There are also individuals who spent significant portions of their lives focused on work, on raising children, or on caring for aging parents or other family members. In those seasons, relationships sometimes took a back seat to everything else that needed attention. The years passed, the responsibilities gradually lifted, and they found themselves with more freedom than they'd had in decades - and no partner to share it with.

Another important factor is that expectations tend to change with experience. Younger people are often willing to take risks in relationships that older people are not. They may overlook real differences because the excitement of the relationship carries them past the warning signs. Later in life, people know themselves better. They know what worked in the past and what didn't. They have a clearer sense of what they will and will not tolerate. That kind of self-awareness is genuinely valuable - but it can also make people more selective in ways that narrow the field considerably.

Sometimes that selectiveness becomes a form of self-protection that operates almost invisibly. After heartbreak or disappointment, a person may decide they are no longer willing to accept certain behaviors or situations. In many ways that's healthy. But it can quietly create a gap between wanting companionship and actually being available for it.

There is also the simple reality that the natural places where people once met potential partners have changed or disappeared. Schools, social gatherings, workplaces - these were the settings where connections formed organically, often without anyone trying particularly hard. Later in life, those environments are largely gone. Social circles tend to shrink rather than expand. Meeting new people requires more deliberate effort than it once did, and for many people that effort feels unfamiliar or even uncomfortable.

One more dynamic is worth naming, because it surprises people who haven't thought about it carefully. By the time someone reaches their fifties or sixties, they have usually built a life they're fairly comfortable in. They have a home arranged the way they like it. Routines that suit them. Habits and preferences that feel natural. Introducing another person into that structure can be appealing in theory and genuinely disruptive in practice. Some people find, when they're honest with themselves, that their independence has become something they value as much as companionship - and that reconciling those two things is harder than they expected.

All of these factors together explain why so many people find themselves single at a stage of life they never imagined they'd reach alone. It is rarely the result of failure or avoidance. More often it is simply what happened - a series of life events, choices, and circumstances that led someone to a place they didn't plan for.

Understanding this matters because it changes the way people think about their situation. Being single later in life does not mean something went wrong. It does not mean a person has missed their chance. It simply means their story took a path that now places them in the position of deciding, perhaps for the first time in a long time, what kind of connection - if any - they want to move toward.

And that decision is almost never made on a clean slate. Everyone who arrives at this point brings something with them. The experiences, the lessons, the emotional residue of the relationships that came before. Understanding what that means - and how to carry it honestly into something new - is where the real conversation begins.

3

DATING WITH BAGGAGE (BECAUSE EVERYONE HAS IT)

The first few dinners between Sandra and Paul had gone well. Conversation came easily. They laughed at the same things. There was a comfort between them that neither had expected to find so quickly. But somewhere around the fourth or fifth time they met, the layers began to show. Paul mentioned, carefully, that his daughter had strong opinions about his dating life and wasn't entirely supportive. Sandra found herself going quiet before she admitted that her finances were still recovering from a divorce settlement that had not gone in her favor. Neither revelation was catastrophic. But the air changed slightly, the way it does when two people realize they are not just meeting each other - they are meeting everything that brought each person to that particular table on that particular evening.

They kept seeing each other. But both of them left that night thinking harder than they had before.

One of the most significant differences between relationships earlier in life and relationships later in life is something people rarely say out loud but almost everyone understands intuitively. By the time someone reaches their fifties, sixties, or beyond, nobody is arriving with a clean slate. Everyone has a past. Everyone carries experiences that shaped them. Everyone brings what people loosely call baggage.

The word itself has picked up an unfairly negative reputation. Baggage suggests drama, dysfunction, or problems waiting to surface. But in the most honest sense, baggage simply means life experience. The longer a person has lived, the more life they have accumulated - relationships, family dynamics, financial decisions, personal struggles, and hard-won lessons about who they are and what they need. None of that can be set aside when someone new walks in the door.

When people are younger, relationships often begin before many of those layers have formed. Two people meet when neither owns a home, neither has children, and neither carries the weight of a complicated history. They build their lives side by side, figuring things out together as they go. Later in life, the situation is fundamentally different. Each person is bringing an entire structure with them - one that was built over decades and is not easily rearranged.

Someone may have adult children who remain central to their daily life. Grandchildren who visit regularly. An ex-spouse still connected through shared family events or ongoing responsibilities. A financial history, a retirement plan, a home they've lived in for twenty years. All of those things become part of the relationship whether they're discussed openly or not. They don't disappear because two people are enjoying each other's company. They simply wait, patiently, until the relationship has developed enough that they can no longer stay in the background.

This is why later-life dating can feel more complicated than people expect. It isn't only about whether two individuals like each other. It's about whether their lives can realistically fit together. Not perfectly — nothing in real life fits perfectly - but well enough that both people can move forward without constantly negotiating the weight of what they've each brought along.

People sometimes underestimate this in the early stages. Initial conversations tend to focus on shared interests, personality, and the simple pleasure of enjoying someone's company. Those things matter deeply. But they're only one layer of a much larger picture. As a relationship develops, the deeper realities of each person's life gradually become visible. A potential partner may have family obligations that consume significant time. Another may carry financial pressures that affect their plans. Some people are still navigating grief, or trust that was damaged by a previous relationship, or a sense of self that is still being rebuilt after years of difficulty.

None of this automatically prevents a relationship from working. Many of the most successful later-life relationships grow precisely from the willingness of two people to understand and respect each other's histories. But they require a level of honesty and self-awareness that younger relationships often don't demand in the same way.

Part of that honesty is directed inward. It's easy to notice another person's complications. It's harder to step back and acknowledge the ways our own history is shaping how we show up. Someone who became guarded after a painful divorce may not fully realize how much that guardedness is influencing the way they respond to a new person trying to get close. Someone who rebuilt their life after a period of real hardship may be more protective of their independence than they understand. Those responses don't come from nowhere - they come from something that happened, something that mattered, something that taught a person to be careful in ways they weren't before.

In some ways, later-life relationships are actually better positioned to handle this honestly than earlier ones were. When two people acknowledge their pasts openly, they have the opportunity to build something grounded in reality rather than romantic projection. They're less likely to pretend they are beginning fresh, because they know too much about life to believe that completely. What they can do instead is learn how to understand each other as complete people - people who have already traveled a long road and arrived carrying everything that road left behind.

That kind of understanding requires patience. It requires real listening. It requires asking questions and being willing to sit with answers that are complicated. But it also makes possible a relationship built on authenticity - one where two people see each other clearly and choose to move forward anyway.

Perhaps the most useful way to think about baggage is not as a liability but as information. Every experience a person has had contributed to who they are today. The painful ones, the joyful ones, the ones they'd rather forget - all of them are part of the story. And when two people explore companionship later in life, they are not simply meeting each other in the present moment. They are meeting the entire journey that delivered each person there.

This also helps dissolve one of the more stubborn fantasies that can attach itself to later-life dating: the idea that somewhere out there is a person who arrives uncomplicated, unburdened, and perfectly suited to step into an already-established life without disturbing a thing. That person almost certainly does not exist. And even if they did, they would be looking at someone else's full life with the same mixture of hope and hesitation.

What matters is not whether someone has a history. Everyone does. What matters is how honestly they carry it, how willing they are to talk about it, and whether two people can understand each other's journeys well enough to build something meaningful - not in spite of those journeys, but partly because of them.

That's the foundation. And understanding what each person is actually bringing to that foundation - the mindset, the emotional posture, the particular way they've learned to approach connection after everything life has shown them - is exactly what the next chapter is about.

4

THE THREE TYPES OF PEOPLE LOOKING FOR COMPANIONSHIP

One of the more interesting things about searching for companionship later in life is that people rarely mean quite the same thing when they say they want a relationship. The words sound the same. The desire sounds the same. But beneath them, the motivations are often very different - and those differences explain why some connections move forward easily while others seem to stall before they ever truly begin.

Over time, a few patterns tend to emerge. While every person is unique, most people searching for companionship in their later years approach it from one of three distinct emotional places. These aren't labels meant to judge or permanently define anyone. They're simply useful ways of understanding what someone might actually be carrying with them when they step back into the world of relationships.

The Rebuilder

Margaret had been divorced for three years when she finally admitted to herself that she missed having someone to share things with. Not the marriage - she had made peace with how that chapter ended. What she missed was simpler. Someone to tell about the odd thing that happened at the grocery store. Someone sitting across the table at dinner who was genuinely interested in how her day went. She wasn't looking to recreate the past. She was looking for something quieter and more honest than what she'd had before.

People like Margaret are Rebuilders. They've been through the hard parts - divorce, loss, long periods of adjustment - and they've come out the other side with something valuable: clarity. Instead of chasing what relationships used to feel like, they're focused on what they actually need now.

Rebuilders tend to ask practical, grounded questions about a potential companion. Can we talk easily? Do we enjoy the same kind of life? Do we treat each other with basic kindness and respect? They're less focused on impressing anyone and more interested in whether two people can genuinely enjoy each other's company over time. Because of this, Rebuilders often make the most natural partners in later-life relationships. They understand that compatibility matters more than chemistry alone, and that the best thing a relationship can offer at this stage isn't excitement - it's peace.

The Replayer

David was sixty-two and, if he was being honest with himself, still thought of himself as the man he'd been at forty. He dressed well, stayed in shape, and had very clear ideas about the kind of woman he wanted to meet. The dates he'd been on had left him underwhelmed. Too quiet, he would say afterward. Not enough spark. What David hadn't quite examined yet was whether the spark he was chasing still fit the life he was actually living.

Replayers are not in any way bad people. The desire to feel vital and attractive doesn't disappear with age, and there's nothing wrong with wanting to feel genuinely alive in a relationship. The challenge is that Replayers are often measuring potential partners against standards that belong to an earlier season of life - standards that may no longer reflect what they actually need to feel genuinely happy.

As a result, Replayers can find themselves caught in a frustrating cycle. They go on dates. They feel disappointed. They wonder why no one seems quite right. But the honest answer is often that they're searching in the present for something that only existed in the past. The relationship they're imagining may have been real once - but the life it belonged to no longer exists in the same form.

The Protector

Carol told anyone who asked that she was fine on her own. And in many ways, she genuinely was. After a long marriage that had slowly worn her down emotionally, and several years spent rebuilding a life she was proud of, she had no interest in going backward. The list of what she required in any potential partner was detailed and firm: financially stable, emotionally self-sufficient, healthy, easy-going, no complications. She had earned the right to be particular, and she knew it. What she hadn't quite admitted to herself was how lonely some evenings had started to feel.

Protectors are people who want companionship but approach it with strong defenses - not out of coldness, but out of hard-won experience. They've often been through genuinely difficult things: betrayal, financial hardship, the exhaustion of caregiving, or years spent recovering from a relationship that took more than it gave. Their caution is earned, and their standards, taken one at a time, are almost always reasonable.

The problem isn't the standards themselves. It's what happens when they stack. When every reasonable requirement is added to the next, the number of people who could realistically qualify grows very small, and the Protector continues waiting for someone who may not exist. More quietly, there's sometimes a deeper function at work: the requirements keep everyone at a safe distance, which means the Protector never has to risk being hurt again.

The Protector often knows this, somewhere beneath the surface. What they need isn't someone to argue them out of their caution. It's enough trust and enough time to lower the drawbridge on their own terms.

When the types meet

What makes later-life dating genuinely complicated is that these three mindsets rarely exist in isolation. A Rebuilder looking for quiet companionship may meet a Replayer still chasing excitement, and both leave the encounter confused about what went wrong. A Protector may be drawn to a Rebuilder's warmth but keep pulling back just as things begin to deepen. Two Protectors might circle each other for months without either one willing to take a real step forward.

Recognizing these patterns doesn't resolve everything, but it helps. It makes it easier to understand that when a connection doesn't develop the way someone hoped, it isn't always about dishonesty or surface-level incompatibility. Sometimes two people simply arrive carrying very different things - and understanding that can replace frustration with something closer to compassion, for the other person and for ourselves.

Most people, if they're honest, will recognize pieces of themselves in more than one category. Someone might approach most situations as a Rebuilder while still carrying a Protector's instincts in certain moments. That isn't a contradiction - it's simply what it looks like to be a person who has lived long enough to collect a few scars alongside the wisdom.

What matters isn't which type fits most accurately. What matters is being honest about the mindset we're bringing into the room — and whether that mindset is moving us toward connection or quietly holding us back from it.

5

WHEN EXPECTATIONS ELIMINATE EVERYONE

The date was going well, by most measures. He was warm, attentive, and made her laugh twice in the first hour. But somewhere between the appetizers and the main course, Patricia's mind had begun doing what it always did. He'd mentioned renting an apartment. She'd noted that quietly. He seemed fit enough, but he'd made an offhand comment about a knee that had been giving him trouble. She'd noted that too. His last relationship had ended badly and he was clearly still processing it - there was that slight heaviness when the subject came up. By the time dessert arrived, the checklist in Patricia's head had done its work. He was kind. He was interesting. He was, she had already decided, not quite right.

She drove home telling herself she had standards for good reasons. Which was true. What she didn't ask herself, not yet, was whether her standards were helping her find someone or simply helping her feel safe from the possibility.

At some point in conversations about relationships later in life, a quiet pattern begins to emerge. Many people say they want companionship. They mean it sincerely. And yet they carry a set of requirements that, taken together, remove most potential partners from consideration before anything real has had a chance to develop. It rarely happens deliberately. The list doesn't appear all at once. It grows slowly, shaped by experience, by disappointment, and by the very reasonable desire not to repeat the things that hurt before.

When someone has lived through a painful divorce, it makes sense that they would become more careful. Someone who spent years in financial stress because of a partner's poor decisions will naturally pay close attention to money matters the next time around. Someone who gave years of their life to caregiving may carry a quiet fear of landing in that position again. Each of those responses is understandable on its own. The problem comes when they accumulate - when every reasonable concern is layered on top of the last until the combined weight of them makes genuine connection nearly impossible.

It often starts simply enough. A person decides they want someone who is financially stable. Fair. Then the person should own their home. Then they should be physically active and in good health. Then free from complicated family dynamics. Then aligned in lifestyle, values, and long-term plans. Each addition seems logical in the moment. But by the time the list is complete, it no longer describes a preference - it describes a person who doesn't exist, or exists in such small numbers that the odds of finding them, let alone connecting with them, are very slim.

What makes this dynamic particularly difficult to see from the inside is that the list always feels justified. Every item on it came from somewhere real. The financial requirement came from a hard lesson. The health concern came from watching someone decline. The insistence on emotional availability came from years spent with someone who wasn't. None of those experiences should be dismissed. But there is a difference between learning from the past and allowing the past to run the entire operation.

There is also something worth examining in the way expectations sometimes function as protection rather than guidance. When the requirements become detailed enough, they create a kind of buffer between a person and the risk of being hurt again. If no one can quite measure up, no one gets close enough to cause damage. The search continues, the standards remain firm, and the loneliness stays at a manageable distance - familiar enough to tolerate, never quite addressed.

This isn't a conscious strategy for most people. It operates quietly, beneath the surface of what feels like reasonable discernment. But it's worth asking honestly whether the expectations we carry are moving us toward connection or doing the opposite - keeping everyone at arm's length while we tell ourselves we simply haven't found the right person yet.

Another layer worth considering is that expectations are often built from an idealized image rather than from real-life experience. People imagine a partner who slides effortlessly into their existing life - present for the good parts, invisible during the private ones, bringing companionship without requiring adjustment. Real relationships do not work that way. Two people with established lives will inevitably encounter differences that require flexibility. The question is whether a person is willing to do that work, or whether they've quietly decided that any relationship requiring adjustment isn't worth pursuing.

There is also a humbling symmetry in all of this. The person doing the evaluating is simultaneously being evaluated. The potential partner sitting across the table has their own list, their own hesitations, their own quiet assessments running in the background. Both people are measuring. Both people are protecting themselves. And both may leave a perfectly good evening having decided the other person wasn't quite right, without either of them fully understanding why.

None of this means lowering every standard or ignoring genuine concerns. Healthy boundaries matter, especially later in life when people have learned through real experience what they can and cannot accept in a relationship. The distinction worth making is between a standard that reflects something truly important and a requirement that exists primarily to keep the door closed.

Sometimes the most useful thing a person can do is sit quietly with that question. Not in a spirit of self-criticism, but honestly. Are the expectations I've built helping me move toward something real? Or have they become, without my quite realizing it, a very sophisticated way of staying exactly where I am?

And then there is the photograph.

Anyone who has spent time on a dating app or website later in life knows exactly what this means without needing it explained. You see a profile. The person looks good. Attractive, put together, younger than you expected. You exchange a few messages. Things feel promising. You agree to meet for coffee.
And then they walk in.

Not that there is anything wrong with the person who walks in. They may be perfectly lovely. But they are clearly not the person in those photographs. The photographs appear to have been taken sometime during the previous administration. Possibly two administrations ago. The hair is different. The face is different. Gravity has been at work in ways the photographs did not capture. You smile, you sit down, and somewhere in the back of your mind you are doing quiet math about what year those pictures might have been taken.

This happens constantly. Men do it. Women do it. Everyone does it and everyone has had it done to them. People post the most flattering photograph they have, which is reasonable enough. But then they post the most flattering photograph they took in 2009, which is something else entirely.

Age is the other version of this. Someone lists themselves as fifty-eight. You meet them and they are clearly sixty-five, which is completely fine, except that it raises an immediate question about what else in the profile might have been adjusted for the market. People shave years off their age the way they used to lie about their weight on a driver's license, as though the truth is somehow going to be less obvious in person than it was on paper.

Here is the thing about all of this. The impulse is understandable. People know that younger photographs attract more attention. They know that a lower age gets more clicks. They are trying to get someone in the door, with the hope that once the person actually meets them, the real connection will take over and the photograph will become irrelevant.

Sometimes that works. More often, the first impression of the meeting is not the person standing in front of you - it is the gap between who you expected and who showed up. And that gap, even when the real person is genuinely wonderful, creates a small cloud of deception that the relationship now has to overcome before it has even ordered coffee.

The honest version is always better. A recent photograph. A real age. An accurate description of what your life actually looks like. The person who responds to that is responding to you - which is the whole point. The person who would have only responded to the 2009 version was never going to work out anyway.

Companionship later in life rarely arrives in perfect packaging. The person who turns out to matter most may not have checked every box at the beginning. They may have a complicated family situation, or a financial history that isn't spotless, or a knee that gives them trouble in cold weather. What they may also have - what often matters far more than any checklist item - is kindness, patience, honesty, and a genuine desire to share the road with someone.

Those qualities are harder to measure on a list. But they are the ones that tend to determine, in the end, whether a relationship actually works.

6

MONEY, PROPERTY, AND HIDDEN EXPECTATIONS

They had been seeing each other for about two months when the subject came up sideways. He mentioned that he'd been thinking about downsizing - the house was more than he needed now that the kids were gone. She said something noncommittal about how that made sense. What neither of them said was what they were actually thinking. She was wondering whether downsizing meant financial pressure she didn't want to inherit. He was wondering whether she expected to eventually share a home, and if so, whose. They talked around it for another twenty minutes before changing the subject entirely, both of them leaving the conversation with the same unresolved questions they'd arrived with.

It would be weeks before they finally said any of it out loud. By then, a small and unnecessary distance had grown between them.

There is a subject that sits quietly in the background of almost every later-life relationship, even when no one is addressing it directly. It isn't romantic. It isn't particularly comfortable. But it shapes the way people evaluate potential partners, the pace at which relationships develop,

and the concerns that linger long after a promising evening has ended. That subject is money.
Not wealth in any flashy sense. Simply stability. Security. The practical question of whether two people's financial lives are compatible enough to share space without creating new problems for each other.

By the time people reach their later years, finances are rarely simple. Most have spent decades working toward some version of stability. They may own a home, carry retirement savings, and have structured their lives in a way that feels secure. That security matters to them - not as a status symbol, but as something they worked hard to build and are not eager to jeopardize. When the possibility of a new relationship enters the picture, financial questions tend to follow close behind, even when they go unspoken.

The questions are rarely asked directly in the early stages. But they are there. People wonder about each other's circumstances without saying so. Do they own or rent? Are they carrying significant debt? Do they have retirement savings, or are they still financially uncertain at a stage of life when uncertainty feels costly? These are not shallow concerns. They often reflect something deeper — a fear of returning to financial stress after years spent escaping it, or a worry about being placed in a position of responsibility for someone else's instability.

For many people, those fears come directly from experience. Someone who spent years in a relationship where money was a constant source of conflict will approach financial questions in the next relationship with heightened sensitivity. Someone who sacrificed their own financial security during a difficult divorce may be particularly protective of what they've managed to rebuild. At this stage of life, there is often less margin for recovery than there once was, and people feel that reality in ways they may not have when they were younger.

There is also a concern that people think about but rarely voice, even to close friends. The question of whether a potential partner is looking for companionship or looking for someone to lean on financially. It isn't a comfortable thing to wonder about another person. It can feel uncharitable, even suspicious. But it is a genuine concern for many people, and pretending otherwise doesn't make it go away. What it does is leave the concern to quietly influence the relationship from underneath rather than being addressed honestly on the surface.

Property adds another layer of complexity that couples earlier in life rarely have to navigate in the same way. When two people have each built a home - arranged it to their taste, settled into the neighborhood, established routines around it - the question of living arrangements becomes surprisingly loaded. One person may feel a deep attachment to their home that goes beyond practicality. Another may have family nearby they are not willing to move away from. In some cases, both individuals prefer to maintain separate homes entirely while still building a meaningful relationship, seeing each other regularly without either person having to give up the life they've created.

This kind of arrangement would have seemed unconventional to many couples a generation ago. Later in life, it has become far more common — and for good reason. It allows two people to enjoy genuine companionship while preserving the independence and personal space they've come to value. It isn't a lesser form of commitment. For many people, it's simply an honest reflection of where they are in life and what they actually need.

Family can complicate financial conversations further still. Adult children often have opinions about a parent's new relationship, particularly when property or inheritance is involved. Even when those opinions are never voiced directly, they can influence how comfortable a person feels about blending their financial life with someone new. Questions about wills, estate planning, and long-term responsibility may not come up in the early months of a relationship, but they tend to surface eventually - and when they do, it helps enormously if both people have already established a foundation of honest communication about practical matters.

That honesty is the thing most people resist and most relationships need. Money is an uncomfortable subject in almost any context, and it becomes more so when it's tangled up with the vulnerability of a new relationship. The instinct is to focus on the emotional connection and let the practical details work themselves out later. Sometimes that works. More often, the details that weren't discussed early become the source of misunderstanding or quiet resentment down the road.

It's worth saying clearly that financial stability does not define a person's worth, and it certainly doesn't determine their capacity for kindness, loyalty, or genuine companionship. People's financial situations are the result of entire life histories - careers that shifted, marriages that ended badly, choices made under circumstances that looked very different at the time. Judging a person solely by their financial standing misses most of what actually matters in a relationship.

At the same time, significant differences in how two people approach money - their spending habits, their comfort with risk, their expectations about sharing expenses - can create real friction if they're never acknowledged. Financial compatibility isn't about matching bank accounts. It's about whether two people's attitudes toward money are compatible enough that the subject doesn't become a recurring source of tension.

Later-life relationships ask people to hold two things at once: the emotional openness that connection requires and the practical awareness that real life demands. Money is not the most romantic part of that conversation. But handled honestly and early, it clears the air in ways that allow everything else to develop on steadier ground.

7

ADULT CHILDREN AND FAMILY DYNAMICS

The first time Diane brought Richard to a family dinner, her daughter was polite in the way that people are when they have decided to be polite rather than warm. She passed the bread. She asked Richard appropriate questions. She laughed once, briefly, at something he said. But later, after Richard had gone home and Diane was helping clear the table, her daughter said quietly that she just wanted to make sure her mother wasn't moving too fast. Diane said she understood. What she didn't say was that she was sixty-one years old, had been alone for four years, and was tired of feeling like she needed permission to be happy.

They didn't fight about it. But the conversation sat between them for a long time afterward, the way those conversations do.

One of the realities that tends to surprise people about relationships later in life is that they are almost never just about two individuals. When someone enters a new relationship at this stage, they are also stepping into a network of existing connections - adult children, grand-children, former spouses, extended family - all of whom have their own feelings about what is happening and their own sense of where they fit in the picture.

Earlier in life, relationships often develop before those structures are fully formed. Two people meet, build a life together, and create their family along the way. The relationship comes first, and everything else grows around it. Later in life, the family structure already exists before the new relationship begins. That reversal changes everything. The new partner isn't arriving at the beginning of a story. They are arriving somewhere in the middle of one, and everyone already in that story has opinions about the new character.

Adult children, in particular, can have complicated reactions. Some are genuinely happy to see a parent find companionship again, especially if that parent has been alone for a long time. They recognize that their parent has a life of their own, that loneliness is real, and that a good companion can make a meaningful difference. These adult children tend to give the relationship room to develop and extend goodwill to the new person even before they know them well.

But not every reaction is this straightforward. Some adult children feel protective, particularly when financial or property matters are involved. They may worry, sometimes with good reason and sometimes without it, about whether a new partner has the right intentions. Those concerns deserve to be acknowledged rather than dismissed - people do sometimes enter relationships with vulnerable older adults for the wrong reasons, and adult children are not wrong to pay attention. The challenge is knowing the difference between reasonable vigilance and emotional resistance dressed up as concern.

That emotional resistance is real and worth understanding with some compassion. Children who grew up watching their parents together carry a powerful internal image of what their family looked like. Even when the previous marriage ended in divorce years ago, or a parent has been widowed for a long time, the sense of family identity can remain surprisingly intact. Seeing a new person step into a significant role in a parent's life can feel like a disruption of something that still feels fundamental - not because the child is selfish, but because family identity runs deeper than people often realize until it is challenged.

There can also be practical anxieties that are harder to talk about openly. Inheritance. Property. The fear that a parent's estate, which children may have quietly assumed would pass to them, could be affected by a new relationship. These concerns don't make adult children villains. But when they go unspoken, they tend to shape behavior in ways nobody fully acknowledges - a coolness that can't quite be explained, a skepticism that seems disproportionate to the situation, an inability to simply be happy for a parent who has found something good.

For the person in the new relationship, navigating all of this can feel exhausting. Building a genuine connection with another person is already vulnerable work. Doing it while also managing the emotions of adult children who may be skeptical or resistant adds a layer of complexity that nobody really prepares people for. A new partner may feel uncertain about their role at family gatherings, unsure how much space they're allowed to occupy, aware that they are being evaluated in ways they can't fully see.

At the same time, it helps to remember that adult children are also adjusting to something unfamiliar. Their resistance, when it exists, usually comes from a place of attachment rather than malice. They are trying to protect something - a parent, a family image, a sense of stability - even if the way they go about it isn't always fair to the people involved. Given time and the right conditions, many families do come around. What often makes the difference is how the situation is handled in the early stages.

Communication tends to be the most powerful tool available. When a parent is open about their new relationship without being defensive, and when they make clear that a new companion is not replacing anyone or erasing what came before, family members often find it easier to adjust. That doesn't mean seeking approval — adults do not need their children's permission to form new relationships. But there is a difference between asking for permission and offering reassurance, and the latter can ease a transition that might otherwise become unnecessarily difficult.

Boundaries matter here too, and they run in both directions. Adult children who are accustomed to a certain level of access to a parent's life may find that a new relationship changes the dynamic — that their parent is less immediately available, more focused on building something new, and no longer quite as centered on the family in the way they once were. Those shifts can feel disorienting. But they are also a natural consequence of a parent reclaiming their own life, which is something adult children should be able to support even when it requires adjustment.

For couples moving through this together, patience and a shared understanding of what each person is dealing with can make an enormous difference. The family dynamics surrounding a later-life relationship rarely resolve quickly. But they do tend to soften over time, particularly when family members can see that the relationship is bringing their parent genuine happiness. Joy, when it's real, is difficult to argue with indefinitely.

In many cases, what begins as tension eventually becomes acceptance, and sometimes something warmer than that. The new partner becomes a familiar presence. The grandchildren grow comfortable. The adult children relax their vigilance when they realize their parent is genuinely cared for. The family circle, rather than being disrupted, quietly expands to make room for someone new.

That outcome isn't guaranteed. But it is more possible than it sometimes feels in the difficult early months - and it almost always depends on the same two things that determine the outcome of most relationship challenges: honesty about what everyone is actually feeling, and the willingness to extend a little more patience than feels strictly necessary.

8

HEALTH, AGING, AND PHYSICAL REALITY

She had stood in front of the mirror longer than usual that morning. Not out of vanity exactly, but out of something harder to name. The date was that evening - the first one in years - and she found herself looking at the face looking back at her with a kind of frank assessment she didn't usually allow. The lines around her eyes. The softness along her jaw that hadn't been there a decade ago. She wasn't unhappy with what she saw. She had lived in this face for sixty-three years and it had served her well. But she wondered, not for the first time, whether the person she was meeting would see what she saw - or whether they would be measuring her against something younger, something she no longer was and had no interest in pretending to be.

She put on her coat and went anyway. But the question stayed with her through dinner, quiet and uninvited, the way those questions do.

There is another subject that runs quietly beneath the surface of many later-life relationships - one that people think about more than they discuss. That subject is health. Not illness specifically, though that's part of it, but the broader reality of what it means to inhabit an aging body while also trying to open yourself to someone new.

When people were younger, health was largely something they took for granted. Energy was abundant. Recovery was quick. The body cooperated without much negotiation. As the years pass, that changes. Not dramatically for everyone, and not all at once, but gradually and unmistakably. Energy levels shift. Certain physical limitations appear. Medical appointments become a more regular feature of life. Bodies that once felt like a given begin to feel more like something that requires attention and care.

None of this is remarkable - it is simply what aging looks like from the inside. But it does influence the way people approach relationships in ways that are worth acknowledging honestly.

Attraction, for one thing, tends to evolve. What people find compelling in a potential companion at sixty is often genuinely different from what drew them at thirty. Physical appearance remains part of the picture, but it tends to carry less singular weight. Vitality matters - the sense that a person is engaged with their life, taking care of themselves, and approaching the years ahead with some degree of energy and intention. Warmth matters. Humor matters. The quality of a person's presence, the way they make someone feel in a conversation, often registers more powerfully than it would have earlier in life when the initial pull of physical attraction could do a lot of the early work on its own. That shift is not a consolation prize. For many people it represents a genuine clarification - a clearer sense of what actually sustains connection over time versus what simply ignites it at the beginning.

Physical differences in energy and lifestyle can still create real questions, though. Someone who loves to travel, hike, or spend long days outdoors naturally hopes to find a companion who can share those experiences. Someone who prefers quieter pleasures - reading, cooking, long conversations over dinner - may feel less compatible with a person whose idea of a good day involves significant physical activity. Neither preference is better. But honest differences in what two people can and want to do with their bodies and their time are worth understanding early, before expectations have formed around an assumption that may not hold.

Health concerns also introduce an emotional dimension that sits deeper than lifestyle compatibility. Many people carry a quiet worry about what illness might eventually require of a relationship - or of them. This fear doesn't usually announce itself directly. It tends to operate in the background, shaping how quickly someone allows a connection to deepen, how much they invest in someone whose health situation is uncertain, and how honestly they talk about their own physical realities.

The fear of becoming a caregiver is a large part of this, and it deserves its own honest acknowledgment. Many people in their fifties and sixties have already spent years in that role - for a parent, for a spouse, for someone they loved and tended through a long decline. That experience leaves a mark. The devotion involved doesn't diminish the difficulty, and some people emerge from it with a very clear sense that they are not willing to enter that particular landscape again. That is not a failure of compassion. It is a human response to something genuinely hard.

At the same time, it's worth remembering that aging is not something a person escapes by remaining single. Health changes happen regardless of whether someone is in a relationship. The question is not whether those changes will come but whether a person wants to face them with a companion beside them or entirely on their own. Framed that way, the calculation looks somewhat different.

There is also the matter of how people feel about themselves physically at this stage of life - something that influences the willingness to be seen in ways that vulnerability requires. Many people become more self-conscious about their appearance as they age, more aware of the distance between how they look now and how they once looked. That self-consciousness can make the early stages of dating feel more exposing than they did in youth, when confidence and physical ease came more naturally.

What tends to happen, though, when two people actually connect, is that those concerns recede. Not because they disappear entirely, but because attention shifts. When someone finds another person genuinely interesting, when the conversation flows and the laughter comes easily and there is a sense of real recognition between two people, the lines around someone's eyes stop registering as something to evaluate. They become simply part of the person - part of the face that has lived a life worth knowing about.

Aging does not eliminate the possibility of attraction or intimacy. It changes the form those things take, and it changes what people are most drawn to in each other. But the capacity for connection - for genuine warmth, for physical closeness, for the particular pleasure of being truly known by another person — does not expire with youth. It simply asks to be met with a little more honesty, a little more patience, and considerably less pretending than it may have required before.

What two people can offer each other at this stage of life is not the same as what they could have offered at thirty. In many ways, what they can offer is better - more considered, more self-aware, more grounded in what actually matters. The body may be different. The understanding of what makes a relationship worth having is usually deeper.

9

SEX AFTER 50, 60, AND BEYOND

It was him who finally said it, about six weeks in, on a quiet evening when they had run out of reasons to keep pretending the subject wasn't there. He said he wanted to be honest with her about something before things went further, and then he told her - carefully, with obvious effort - about the medication he'd been on for the past two years and what it sometimes meant for him physically. He watched her face while he talked. She didn't look away. When he finished, she was quiet for a moment, and then she said that she appreciated him telling her, and that she had a few things she'd been wanting to say too. They talked for a long time that night. It wasn't the most comfortable conversation either of them had ever had. It was, both of them agreed later, one of the most important.

There is perhaps no subject more present in the minds of people navigating relationships later in life, and less openly discussed, than sexuality. It gets skirted around. It gets implied. It occasionally gets addressed in the careful, clinical language of health articles. But the honest, human conversation - the one that acknowledges that sex and intimacy remain part of many people's lives well into their later years, and that navigating those things with someone new after decades of experience is its own complicated and sometimes tender territory - that conversation is rarer than it should be.

Part of the reason is cultural. There is an unspoken assumption in much of society that desire belongs primarily to the young, and that sexuality among older adults is either nonexistent or vaguely inappropriate as a subject of open discussion. That assumption is not only wrong - it is genuinely unhelpful to the millions of people for whom intimacy remains an important part of how they experience connection and feel close to another person.

The reality is that sexual desire does not simply switch off at a certain age. For many people it continues, though it may change in character and intensity. For others it becomes less central over time, replaced by other forms of closeness that feel equally meaningful. Both experiences are real and both deserve to be treated as normal rather than as something to hide or apologize for.

What does change, for most people, is the body. And the body's changes are worth discussing honestly rather than dancing around. For women, menopause introduces a set of physical realities that can affect sexual experience in significant ways. Hormonal shifts may reduce libido, create physical discomfort, or change the way the body responds to intimacy. These are not permanent sentences - many women find ways to navigate them effectively, with or without medical support - but they are real, and they can make the prospect of sexual vulnerability with someone new feel considerably more complicated than it did in earlier years. A woman who is uncertain about how her body will respond, or who carries some self-consciousness about those changes, may find the early stages of physical intimacy genuinely anxiety-producing in ways her younger self never experienced.

For men, the most common challenges involve erectile dysfunction and changes in sexual response - both of which are far more prevalent than the silence around them might suggest. A significant number of men over fifty experience these issues to some degree. They are in most cases manageable, often treatable, and almost universally embarrassing to talk about. The embarrassment is understandable. The silence it produces is not always helpful. When a man is unable to have an honest conversation with a new partner about what his body may or may not do, misunderstanding tends to fill the space that honesty would have occupied - and misunderstanding, in that particular context, can do real damage to a connection that was otherwise developing well.

This is where communication becomes not just useful but essential. Two people who can talk honestly about their physical realities - what they're comfortable with, what concerns them, what their bodies are doing and not doing - are in a far better position than two people who are trying to navigate intimacy while simultaneously managing unspoken fears and unaddressed expectations. Those conversations are not always easy to initiate. They require a degree of trust that may still be developing, and a willingness to be seen in a vulnerable way that many people find more difficult at this stage of life than they expected.

The vulnerability is real. After years of knowing one person's body and being known by them, the prospect of physical intimacy with someone new can feel genuinely exposing. There is no accumulated history to fall back on, no established shorthand, no quiet confidence that comes from long familiarity. Everything is new again, and new, at this age, can feel less exciting and more frightening than it once did.

What many people discover, though, is that intimacy later in life can develop a quality that was harder to access when they were younger. The pressure that often accompanied sex in earlier years - to perform, to impress, to meet some internal or external standard - tends to ease with age. When two people are less focused on how they appear and more focused on how they feel, physical closeness can become something genuinely mutual in a way it wasn't always before. The goal shifts from performance to presence. And presence, it turns out, is often what people wanted all along.

It is also important to acknowledge that not everyone wants sexual intimacy to be a central part of a later-life relationship, and that this is equally valid. Some people find that what they most desire at this stage is companionship, emotional closeness, and physical affection - holding hands, being held, the warmth of another person nearby - without sex playing a significant role. For them, that is not a diminished version of intimacy. It is simply an honest reflection of where they are.

What becomes a genuine problem is when two people have different expectations about the role of sexuality in their relationship and neither has said so. One person may consider physical intimacy central to feeling truly connected. The other may feel the relationship is already complete without it. When that gap goes unaddressed, it tends to generate a specific kind of tension - one that both people feel and neither quite names - that can quietly erode something that might otherwise have been strong.

The solution, as with most things in later-life relationships, is the conversation that feels most difficult to start. Not a clinical negotiation, and not a formal declaration, but an honest exchange between two people who have decided they trust each other enough to say what is actually true. Those conversations, when they happen, almost always bring people closer rather than further apart - even when, or perhaps especially when, what gets said is complicated.

Society may not encourage older adults to speak openly about their sexual lives. But the people living those lives know that intimacy, in whatever form it takes, remains one of the ways human beings feel most genuinely connected to each other. Pretending otherwise doesn't protect anyone. It simply leaves people navigating something important entirely alone when they don't have to be.

Later-life relationships that include physical intimacy are not trying to recreate the experiences of youth. They are discovering what closeness means for two specific people at a specific point in their lives - with all the history, self-knowledge, and hard-won honesty that this particular moment makes possible. When approached that way, intimacy at this stage can be less fraught and more genuine than it was in earlier years. Not louder. Not more dramatic. But often, quietly, more real.

10

THE FEAR OF BECOMING A CAREGIVER

For three years, Frank had taken care of his wife. He had done it without complaint and without regret, because she was the person he loved and there was never really a question of whether he would. But he also knew, in the honest part of himself he didn't always visit, what those years had cost him. The exhaustion that went deeper than sleep could fix. The slow disappearance of his own needs beneath the weight of hers. The particular loneliness of being the person in the room who was not allowed to fall apart. When she passed, he grieved fully and genuinely. And then, after a year or so, he began to think about companionship again - and found, to his own surprise, that the thought was immediately followed by another one, quieter and less comfortable: I don't know if I can do that again.

He didn't say this to anyone for a long time. It felt disloyal, somehow. Like a betrayal of everything those years had meant.

There is a concern that many people carry into the conversation about later-life relationships that rarely gets named directly. It doesn't announce itself as a fear. It tends to present as practicality, as wisdom, as a reasonable assessment of what relationships at this stage of life might eventually require. But underneath the careful language, the concern is real and it is human: the possibility of becoming a caregiver.

As people grow older, they become more aware - through personal experience, through watching friends and family, through the simple accumulation of years - that health can change. Illness arrives. Mobility decreases. Conditions that were manageable become consuming. And when someone has already lived through the experience of caring for another person through a serious decline, the idea of entering a new relationship carries a weight it might not carry for someone who hasn't been through that particular passage.

This is not a failure of compassion. It needs to be said clearly, because people often feel guilty for having this fear at all. They tell themselves that a loving person wouldn't hesitate, that the fear makes them selfish, that they should be willing to accept whatever a relationship might eventually require. But caregiving is genuinely one of the most demanding things a human being can take on. The people who do it well - who show up day after day, who set aside their own needs, who carry both the practical weight and the emotional one - understand in their bodies what it costs in ways that are difficult to convey to someone who hasn't experienced it firsthand.

When someone has given that much of themselves once, the prospect of doing it again is not a small thing to consider. It is a large thing. And pretending otherwise, in the name of seeming generous or open-hearted, doesn't serve anyone honestly.
At the same time, the fear deserves to be examined rather than simply obeyed. Because there are a few things worth holding alongside it.

The first is that aging happens regardless. A person who remains single in order to avoid the possibility of caregiving may still find themselves facing their own health challenges without a companion to offer support. The arrangement they feared becoming - one person caring for another - is not unique to romantic relationships. It is simply the shape that love sometimes takes when life gets hard. The question is not whether that shape will ever appear but who, if anyone, will be present when it does.

The second is that caregiving in a later-life relationship does not necessarily look the way it did the last time. Many people's caregiving experiences happened within marriages where the expectation of total commitment was absolute and help from outside the relationship was limited or unavailable. The landscape has shifted. Community resources, healthcare support, and family networks can provide assistance in ways that make the burden more distributed and more manageable. A new relationship, particularly one entered into by two people who have talked honestly about expectations and limits, does not have to replicate the experience that left someone depleted before.

The third is that the fear, when it goes unexamined, can operate as a quiet veto on connection that the person holding it may not fully intend. Someone can genuinely want companionship while simultaneously keeping every potential partner at the precise distance required to ensure they never have to find out what the relationship might eventually ask of them. That is a coherent response to real pain. It is also, over time, a form of isolation that doesn't announce itself as such.

What tends to help is conversation - honest, specific, and earlier than feels comfortable. When two people can talk about their health situations, their histories with caregiving, and what they would and would not be able to offer each other if circumstances changed, the abstract fear becomes a concrete discussion. Concrete discussions have answers, or at least directions. Abstract fears tend only to grow.

None of this resolves the fear entirely. Some people will weigh everything honestly and still decide that the risk is more than they are willing to take, and that is a legitimate choice that deserves respect. Others will find that naming the fear out loud - to themselves and eventually to a potential partner - reduces its power over the decision considerably.

What almost everyone eventually comes to understand is that later-life relationships involve accepting a degree of uncertainty that cannot be fully managed. Two people cannot know what the future will ask of them. What they can know is whether they trust each other enough to face whatever comes, and whether the connection they share is strong enough to make that uncertainty feel like something worth navigating together rather than something to be avoided at all costs.

That is not a guarantee. But it is, for many people, enough.

11

WHEN FAMILY BECOMES THE SUBSTITUTE FOR PARTNERSHIP

After the second year of half-hearted dates and disappointing evenings, Carolyn stopped renewing her subscription to the dating site. She didn't make a decision exactly - there was no moment of resolution, no firm conclusion reached. She simply let it lapse and found, to her own mild surprise, that she felt relief rather than loss. She redirected her energy toward her grandchildren, toward her sister who lived forty minutes away, toward the garden and the book club and the rhythms of a life that was, by any fair measure, full. She told herself she was content. Most of the time, she was. It was only occasionally - on a Sunday evening, perhaps, or during a long drive alone - that she noticed something underneath the contentment that she didn't look at too closely.

She wasn't unhappy. She simply wasn't quite finished with the question she'd decided to stop asking.

There is a pattern that develops quietly in the lives of many people as the search for companionship becomes more difficult or more discouraging than they anticipated. Without quite deciding to, they begin to shift. The energy that once went toward meeting new people, navigating dating, and holding open the possibility of a new relationship gradually redirects itself toward the connections already present - children, grandchildren, siblings, old friends. The family becomes the center. And in many ways, that is a natural and even beautiful thing.

Family relationships can bring deep and genuine fulfillment. Many people build rich, meaningful lives centered entirely around those bonds, and they are not compensating for anything or settling for less than what they truly wanted. For them, family is not a substitute. It is the genuine article, and the idea that something is missing simply doesn't apply.

But for others, the shift toward family carries a quieter undertone — one that isn't always examined honestly. The investment in family life becomes, at least in part, a way of filling a space that once held the possibility of something else. It can feel safer that way. Family connections carry a familiarity and a stability that a new relationship cannot offer. The vulnerability required to open yourself to someone unknown, the frustration of expectations unmet, the particular exhaustion of trying again after previous disappointment - none of that is required with family. The love is already established. The effort feels different.

This is understandable. It deserves to be said plainly rather than treated as something to overcome or correct. When the search for companionship has been discouraging enough for long enough, redirecting toward what is already solid and real is not weakness. It is a reasonable response to repeated difficulty.

What is worth examining honestly, though, is whether the shift represents a genuine change in what a person wants or a practical accommodation to what feels achievable. Those are different things, and conflating them can leave someone living a life that looks complete from the outside while something quiet and persistent continues underneath.

The distinction matters in part because family relationships and romantic companionship occupy genuinely different spaces in a person's life. Children, no matter how devoted, have their own lives to lead. They have careers, partners, and children of their own. The time and attention they can offer a parent is real but limited by the natural demands of their own adulthood. Grandchildren bring a particular kind of joy that is difficult to describe and impossible to replicate - but they grow up, move forward, and eventually need their grandparents in different and diminishing ways.

A companion, by contrast, is present in the texture of ordinary days. They are there on Tuesday evening when nothing particular is happening. They notice small things. They are woven into the routine rather than arriving for the occasions. That quality of presence is different from what family provides - not more important, but different in a way that matters to many people once they allow themselves to acknowledge it.

There is also sometimes a dimension of self-sacrifice at work that is worth naming. Some people pull back from the search for companionship not because they have stopped wanting it but because they worry about how a new relationship might affect the family. They have watched adult children react with discomfort or resistance to the idea of a new partner, and they have decided, quietly and without saying so, that keeping the peace is worth more than pursuing what they want for themselves. They fold their own desires into the background and present the family as the reason rather than the obstacle.

That choice is sometimes genuinely right for a specific person in a specific situation. But it is worth making consciously rather than drifting into it, because the difference between choosing family and surrendering to pressure is significant - both in terms of how a person feels about their life and in terms of what remains unspoken and unresolved between them and the people they love.

For people who have genuinely arrived at contentment with a life centered on family and independence, none of this is a challenge or a correction. It is simply an acknowledgment that their path is valid. What matters most, at every stage of this conversation, is honesty with oneself about what is actually true - not what seems acceptable to say, not what appears easiest to maintain, but what is genuinely present underneath.

Because the search for connection, when it is real, does not entirely go away simply because a person has decided to stop looking. It tends to wait. It surfaces on quiet evenings and long drives. It sits in the background of full and otherwise satisfying days. And recognizing it honestly - rather than explaining it away - is usually the first step toward understanding what, if anything, a person actually wants to do about it.

12

COMPANIONSHIP VS. ROMANTIC LOVE

She had liked him from the beginning. He was thoughtful and funny and easy to be around, and after several months of seeing each other regularly she found herself looking forward to his company in a way that had become part of the reliable texture of her week. But one evening, sitting across from him at a restaurant they had been to several times before, she caught herself thinking something she hadn't expected. She wasn't in love with him - not in the way she remembered love feeling when she was younger, not with that particular urgency and preoccupation. What she felt was something quieter. She was comfortable with him. She trusted him. She genuinely enjoyed being in his presence in a way that had nothing to do with drama or longing.

For a moment she wondered if that meant something was wrong. Then she thought about it a little longer and decided it might actually mean something was right.

One of the most important realizations many people arrive at later in life is that companionship and romantic love are not the same thing - and that understanding the difference between them is often the key to finding what they actually need rather than continuing to search for something that belongs to an earlier chapter.

When people are younger, relationships tend to be built around a particular kind of emotional intensity. Love, in that stage of life, can feel consuming. It arrives with urgency, with preoccupation, with the sense that the world has rearranged itself around another person. That experience is real and it is valuable. But it is also, at least in part, a product of where people are in their lives - the openness of youth, the novelty of early experience, the particular energy that comes from building a future that hasn't yet taken shape.

Later in life, something shifts. Not because people become less capable of feeling deeply, but because what they most need from a relationship has genuinely changed. The future has largely been shaped. The family has been built or not built. The career has run its course or is running it. The major structures of a life are in place. What people are looking for now is not someone to build with, but someone to be present with - and that is a different thing entirely.

Companionship is quieter than romantic love. It does not announce itself with the same force. It is built on comfort and trust and the particular ease that develops between two people who have chosen, consistently and without drama, to show up for each other. A companion is someone whose presence feels natural rather than electric. Conversations flow without effort. Silence doesn't require filling. Time spent together has a quality of simple rightness that is less about excitement and more about something steadier - the feeling of being genuinely at home with another person.

For many people, this realization arrives with a certain amount of confusion. They were taught, implicitly or explicitly, that love is supposed to feel a particular way - intense, transformative, unmistakable. When a relationship develops that feels warm and solid and genuinely good without producing that specific feeling, people sometimes wonder whether it counts. Whether they are settling. Whether something essential is missing.

What is usually missing is not the relationship. What is missing is the framework for understanding that a different kind of connection can be equally real and equally valuable. Companionship is not romantic love with the passion removed. It is its own form of closeness - one that often grows more durable over time precisely because it is not dependent on a particular emotional temperature being maintained.

This does not mean that romance disappears from later-life relationships entirely. Many couples in their sixties and beyond still experience genuine affection, physical closeness, and moments that carry real tenderness and warmth. The difference is that these expressions of love tend to be woven into the broader fabric of companionship rather than standing alone as the primary measure of the relationship's health. A long conversation on a Sunday morning, a hand held without thinking about it, the quiet satisfaction of doing ordinary things alongside someone who understands you - these become the currency of connection, and they are worth more than they are often given credit for.

There is also a certain freedom in recognizing this distinction clearly. When companionship becomes the honest goal rather than a concession to the goal that didn't materialize, people stop measuring their relationships against an emotional standard that was never going to apply. They stop waiting to feel something that may not be coming and start paying attention to what is actually present. And what is present, when two people genuinely enjoy each other's company and have chosen each other thoughtfully, is often more than enough.

Some relationships that begin as companionship deepen over time into something that resembles love in the fullest sense - not the urgent love of youth, but the kind that develops slowly from familiarity and care and the accumulated weight of shared experience. It is a love that knows the other person completely and has decided to stay anyway.

Many people find, looking back, that this is the love they are most grateful for - not because it was the most intense, but because it was the most true.

Understanding the difference between companionship and romantic love is not about lowering expectations. It is about replacing the wrong expectations with the right ones. The right question to ask about a potential companion is not whether they produce a particular feeling but whether they make ordinary life feel better. Whether the days are easier with them in them. Whether their presence adds something real and consistent and good.

That, for many people in the later seasons of life, is exactly what love has become.

13

MERGING TWO ALREADY-BUILT LIVES

The first time he stayed at her place for an entire weekend, they both discovered things they hadn't expected. She liked the kitchen arranged a specific way and noticed, without saying anything, that he had moved things while making breakfast. He was an early riser who found the silence of the morning essential, and she preferred to ease into the day slowly with the television on for company. Neither of these things was a serious problem. But on Sunday evening, after he had driven home and she was putting the kitchen back the way she preferred it, she found herself thinking about what it would actually mean - practically, daily, in the small and ordinary ways that don't come up in restaurants and on walks - to share a life with someone who had spent decades becoming very comfortable with his own way of doing things.

As, she acknowledged to herself, had she.

One of the quiet discoveries people make when a later-life relationship begins to develop seriously is that the logistics are more complicated than they anticipated. The emotional connection may be genuine. The companionship may feel exactly right. And yet, somewhere in the background, the practical question begins to take shape: how do two lives that are already fully formed actually come together without one or both of them losing something essential?

It is a question that younger couples rarely have to ask in the same way. When people meet early in adulthood, their lives are still being built. Habits are flexible. Homes are temporary. Routines are improvised rather than established. Two people can grow into a shared life relatively naturally because neither of them has yet grown too far into a separate one. Later in life, the situation is fundamentally different. The habits are not improvised - they are deeply worn. The home is not temporary - it is a place someone has lived in for years, possibly decades, and arranged to reflect exactly who they are. The routines are not flexible - they are the architecture of a daily life that feels comfortable precisely because it has been refined over time.

When two people with that kind of established life try to build something together, they are not starting from a blank page. They are trying to find the places where two already-finished pages might overlap without obscuring what's already written on either one.

Living arrangements tend to be the first place this becomes concrete. If both people own homes they are attached to, the question of where to live carries a weight it simply wouldn't have at thirty. A home later in life is rarely just a building. It is a neighborhood where someone knows their neighbors. It is the proximity to children or grandchildren who live nearby. It is years of accumulated comfort - the particular way light falls through a window in the morning, the garden that has been tended season after season, the spare room that became something specific and irreplaceable over time. Asking someone to leave all of that is asking for something significant, and both people in the relationship usually understand that on some level even when neither says it directly.

This is one of the reasons that maintaining separate homes while building a genuine relationship has become an increasingly common arrangement among people who meet later in life. It is sometimes described with a faint note of apology, as though it represents a reluctance to fully commit. In reality, for many people it represents something more honest - an acknowledgment that two people can be genuinely important to each other without either of them having to sacrifice the life they worked to build. They spend meaningful time together. They are present for each other in the ways that matter. They simply also retain the personal space and independence that allows each of them to remain fully themselves.

There is no single right answer to how two established lives should be arranged. What matters is that both people are honest about what they need rather than performing a version of commitment that doesn't fit the reality of who they actually are.

Daily routines present their own set of adjustments, quieter but equally real. People who have lived alone for years - or who managed their own households for decades - tend to have very specific relationships with their own time and space. The morning belongs to them in a particular way. The evening unfolds according to habits that have become almost unconscious. When another person enters that structure, even someone welcome and genuinely cared for, the disruption can be more significant than expected. Small things surface. One person needs quiet to think; the other fills space with sound. One keeps a kitchen one way; the other has a different system that makes equal sense to them. Neither habit is wrong. But two habits occupying the same space require negotiation, and negotiation, even between people who like each other very much, requires patience and a willingness to relinquish some of the control that comes with living entirely on one's own terms.

Financial planning adds another dimension. By the time people reach their fifties and sixties, they have made significant financial decisions -

about property, retirement, savings, and the long-term shape of their estates - that cannot simply be set aside when a new relationship begins. Deciding how to handle shared expenses, how to approach property, and how to think about the financial future together requires conversations that many couples delay far longer than is helpful. The discomfort is understandable. Money and love feel like they belong in separate categories. But in practice they occupy the same life, and the couples who navigate this well tend to be the ones who addressed it early and directly rather than letting it accumulate into a source of unspoken tension.

Family connections shape the texture of merged lives as well. Both people likely have established traditions - holidays spent certain ways, weekends that belong to grandchildren, routines built around family that have been in place for years. Integrating a new partner into those structures takes time and sensitivity, and it rarely happens all at once. Some traditions will adapt. Others may remain unchanged because changing them would cost too much. Finding a balance that honors what already exists while making room for what is being built requires ongoing attention from both people, not just in the early months but throughout the life of the relationship.

What makes all of this worthwhile is what two fully developed people actually bring to each other. They are not arriving with potential that has yet to be realized. They are arriving with a lifetime of experience, perspective, and accumulated depth that has already been realized. The conversations are richer because both people have lived long enough to have something genuinely considered to say. The shared appreciation for ordinary pleasures - a good meal, an evening walk, an unhurried morning - carries a quality of awareness that comes from understanding, through actual experience, how easily those pleasures can disappear.

Two people who have each spent decades becoming who they are bring something to a relationship that youth, for all its energy and possibility, cannot replicate. They bring the fullness of a life already lived. The challenge of merging two established lives is real. But so is the reward that waits on the other side of the effort - a companionship that is not being constructed from raw materials but assembled from two lifetimes of careful and deliberate becoming.

14

LEARNING TO SHARE THE LATER SEASONS OF LIFE

They had been together for almost two years when she realized, one October afternoon, that she had stopped keeping track. They were walking along a path they had walked before, not talking about anything in particular - something about the neighbor's dog, something about whether it would rain before they got back - and she noticed that she felt entirely at ease. Not happy in any dramatic sense. Simply at ease, in the deep and quiet way that takes a long time to arrive and is, when it finally does, worth more than most of the louder things that came before it.

She had not expected, at sixty-seven, to feel this particular feeling again. She was glad she had left the door open long enough for it to find her.

One of the most useful ways to understand relationships later in life is to recognize that life itself moves through seasons. Not metaphorically, in the vague way people sometimes mean when they use that word, but genuinely and structurally - each stage of life carrying its own particular character, its own priorities, and its own way of understanding what connection means and what it asks of us.

The spring of life is a time of discovery. Everything is forming. People are learning who they are, what they want, and what kind of life they hope to build. Relationships in this season are shaped by possibility - two people coming together before much has been settled, drawn by the energy of a future that is still entirely open. There is an excitement to that, and a particular kind of hope that belongs specifically to beginnings.

Summer brings the long work of building. Careers take shape. Families grow. Responsibilities multiply and deepen. Relationships in this season are closely tied to the shared project of constructing an adult life - raising children, maintaining a home, working toward goals that are years in the making. There is momentum to this season, and a sense of forward motion that can make the days feel both full and fast.

Fall arrives when many of those responsibilities begin to shift and settle. Children have grown. Careers are winding toward their conclusion or have already reached it. The urgent work of building is largely done, and something different takes its place - a quieter kind of attention, turned less toward the future and more toward the present. People begin to ask questions they had little time for before. What truly matters now? What kind of life do I want in the years I have remaining? Who do I want to share them with?

This is the season in which the search for companionship often becomes most meaningful. Not because love was absent in the earlier seasons, but because what people are looking for has changed in ways that only become clear from here. The goal is no longer to find someone to build with. It is to find someone to be present with - someone who understands the road that led to this particular moment, because they have traveled a version of it themselves.

Eventually, life moves into its winter. This season is often misread as one of diminishment - a trailing off, a gradual subtraction. But winter has its own quality, distinct from the others and not lesser than them. It is a time of reflection and of depth, of appreciation sharpened by the awareness that time is finite and that the ordinary moments of life are not as ordinary as they once appeared.

Relationships in this season carry a different kind of tenderness. Two people who share their winter understand each other in a way that requires no explanation, because they are both living the same truth - that what remains is valuable precisely because it will not remain forever.

Understanding these seasons matters because so much of the difficulty people experience in later-life relationships comes from carrying the expectations of one season into another. Someone who is searching in their sixties for the intensity and urgency that characterized relationships in their twenties is not looking for what this season actually offers. They are looking backward. And what is available here - the ease, the depth, the quiet satisfaction of genuine companionship - goes unrecognized because it doesn't look like what they remember wanting.

When people release those earlier expectations and allow themselves to want what this season can actually provide, something often opens up. The connections available in the later years are not consolation prizes for what youth offered and is now gone. They are different gifts - ones that require a longer life to be ready to receive.

Sharing the later seasons of life with someone is not about recreating an earlier chapter. It is about writing a new one, with the full weight of everything both people have lived informing every page. The conversations carry more because each person has more to bring to them. The silences are more comfortable because neither person needs to fill them with performance. The ordinary moments - a shared meal, an afternoon that goes nowhere in particular, the reliable presence of someone who has chosen to stay - carry a significance that is felt rather than announced.

There is also something particular about the way imperfection settles into acceptance in this season. By the time two people reach this stage of life they have seen enough of the world to know that nobody arrives whole and uncomplicated. Everyone has their edges, their habits, their ways of being that don't always accommodate another person easily. Relationships in the later years, at their best, are ones where both people have decided that those imperfections are not obstacles but simply the texture of a real human being - and that the real human being beside them is worth the texture.

That acceptance does not come automatically or without effort. It is the product of patience, of choosing to understand rather than judge, of returning to the relationship again and again with the decision that it is worth tending. But when it settles in, it creates something that the more dramatic forms of connection rarely produce: a steadiness that holds in all weather, not because the weather is always fair, but because the foundation beneath it was built carefully and with clear eyes.

These later seasons may not carry the electricity of earlier ones. They carry something else instead - a warmth that doesn't flare and go out, a companionship that knows what it is and has stopped pretending to be anything other than that. For many people, looking back across all the seasons they have moved through, it is this one they are most grateful for.

And it begins, as every season does, simply by being willing to live in it fully - to stop looking over one shoulder at what has passed and turn, instead, toward whoever might be walking beside you now.

15

IS THERE REALLY SOMEBODY FOR EVERYBODY?

There is a moment that many people describe, somewhere in the later years, when the question they grew up hearing - there's somebody for everybody - surfaces again with a different weight than it carried before. Not as a comfort exactly. More as something to be reckoned with honestly. They find themselves sitting with it the way you sit with a question that deserves a real answer rather than the one that was always given, and they realize that what they are actually asking is something slightly different from what the phrase says. Not whether a specific person exists somewhere, waiting. But whether connection - real, ordinary, sustaining connection - is still possible for them. Whether that door is still open. Whether they are.

By the time people reach the later seasons of life, most of them have seen enough of the world to know that relationships do not follow the neat and reassuring patterns that phrase once suggested. Some people remain in the same marriage their entire lives and find it genuinely good. Others experience divorce, loss, long stretches of solitude, and the particular kind of starting over that nobody plans for when they are young. Some find new companions later in life. Others build something full and meaningful without a romantic partner at the center of it. Life, it turns out, is considerably less tidy than the saying implied. Which means the question of whether there is somebody for everybody may not have a single answer. And it may not be the most useful question to carry.

What becomes clearer with time - and this is one of the things that only the later seasons of life can teach - is that companionship is not primarily a matter of destiny. It is a matter of openness. Of the choices people make about how available they are willing to be, how honestly they are willing to see themselves and others, and how much of the self-protection they have accumulated over the years they are willing to set aside in the service of something real.

Some people remain genuinely open. They have been hurt and they carry the evidence of that, but they have not closed around it. They are willing to be surprised. They hold their requirements loosely enough that a real person can fit through them. And they tend, over time, to find connection - not because the universe reserved someone for them, but because they kept the conditions for connection alive in themselves.

Others close, gradually and often without realizing it. The requirements stack. The defenses settle into permanence. The desire for companionship remains real but operates at a distance from any actual willingness to be vulnerable, and the gap between wanting connection and allowing it widens until the two are no longer in conversation with each other. These people are not failures. They are, in most cases, people who were hurt enough that closing felt like the only reasonable response. But the closing has a cost, and it is worth naming.

The truth that sits underneath the familiar phrase is not that every person is guaranteed a specific partner. It is that every person retains the capacity for connection - for being known, for knowing someone else, for the particular warmth that passes between two people who have decided to show up honestly for each other. That capacity does not expire. It can be buried, and it can be protected to the point of suffocation, but it does not disappear simply because time has passed or because the road here was harder than expected.

For those who continue searching, it helps enormously to carry realistic expectations - not lowered ones, but honest ones. The companion worth finding is not the one who arrives without complications or history or the accumulated weight of a fully lived life. That person does not exist. The companion worth finding is the one whose complications can coexist peacefully with your own. Whose history you can respect even when you don't share it. Whose presence in the ordinary days of your life makes those days feel less like something to get through and more like something worth having.

Companionship later in life can also take forms that don't fit the traditional picture, and it is worth being genuinely open to that. Two people who maintain separate homes and build something real between them. A relationship that centers on friendship and shared experience without the formal structures that defined earlier partnerships. Connections that develop slowly from unlikely beginnings and become, over time, the most important ones. Life at this stage offers fewer scripts and more actual freedom than many people recognize - freedom to define what connection means rather than measuring everything against a template that may never have fit perfectly in the first place.

And for those who arrive at a place of genuine contentment without a romantic partner - who have built lives rich with friendship, family, community, and personal meaning - that too is a real and valid answer to the question. Not a consolation. Not a settling. A life that found its fullness through a different arrangement than the one the old saying described.

Perhaps what the phrase is really reaching for, underneath its simplicity, is something like this: that no person is beyond the possibility of connection. That the human capacity for love and companionship and genuine recognition of another person does not have a natural expiration date. That the later seasons of life, for all their complications and losses and accumulated weight, do not close that possibility - they simply ask it to take a more honest form than it may have required before.

Whether there is literally somebody for everybody remains, in the end, an open question. But the possibility of connection - of being known, of sharing the days with someone who understands the road you traveled to get here - remains one of the most enduring and most human things there is.

And it remains available, for as long as a person is willing to remain available to it.

A FINAL HONEST CONVERSATION

THE MIRROR NOBODY WANTS TO LOOK IN

There is one more thing worth saying before this book closes, and it is probably the one thing most people will resist the most. Not because it isn't true, but because it is true in a way that is uncomfortable to sit with.

Many people who say they cannot find anyone worth their time have never stopped to ask honestly whether they themselves are what they are looking for.

That is not a cruel observation. It is a fair one.

Think about how the search actually works. A person builds their list. They know what they want. Financial stability. Good health. Emotional availability. No complicated baggage. An attractive, put-together individual who fits easily into a well-organized life. They hold that list up to everyone they meet and measure accordingly. What they rarely do is turn that same list around and hold it up to themselves.

Are they financially stable, or are they still carrying debt and uncertainty while requiring security from someone else? Are they healthy and active, or have they let themselves go while expecting a partner who has not? Are they emotionally available, or are they still guarded, still processing old wounds, still keeping everyone at arm's length while wondering why no one gets close? Are they free from baggage, or are they walking in with a full set of luggage and expecting the other person to carry it without complaint?

Most people evaluate potential partners based on what they hope to receive. They present themselves based on who they used to be. There is a significant difference between those two things, and most people know it when they see it in someone else and are completely blind to it in themselves.

Here is something that researchers who study dating behavior have found consistently, and that anyone who has spent time in the dating world later in life will recognize immediately: people routinely pursue partners who are out of their realistic range - in attractiveness, in status, in lifestyle - and then feel genuinely puzzled and hurt when those people are not interested. At the same time, they are often dismissing people at their own level without a second look. The result is a cycle of frustration that has less to do with the available pool of partners and more to do with a self-image that has not caught up with reality.

This happens to everyone to some degree. It is human. But it becomes more pronounced later in life because people are often measuring themselves against a version of who they were twenty or thirty years ago. The man who was considered very attractive and successful at forty-five may still be operating from that self-image at sixty-eight, presenting requirements as though the person the other side of the table is getting is that forty-five year old. They are not. They are getting a sixty-eight year old with a complicated history, health realities, adult children, and all the other things he is quietly disqualifying everyone else for having.

None of this is said to be unkind. It is said because the people reading this book have earned the honest version of this conversation.

The same generosity people hope someone will extend to them - the willingness to look past imperfections, to value what is genuinely good in a person, to see the whole human being rather than the checklist - that generosity has to travel in both directions. You cannot hold others to a standard of patience and understanding that you are not willing to apply to yourself. You cannot ask someone to see past the complications in your life while refusing to see past the complications in theirs.

There is also something quieter underneath this worth naming. When people set the bar very high for everyone around them, it sometimes has less to do with genuine standards and more to do with never wanting to be chosen. If the requirements are impossible to meet, nobody ever gets close enough to see the parts of ourselves we are not sure anyone would want. The high bar is not always about finding the best person. Sometimes it is about making sure no person can ever quite reach us.

Looking in that mirror honestly is not comfortable. But it is one of the most useful things a person can do before stepping back into the search for companionship. Not to tear themselves down. Not to decide they are not worthy of what they want. But to make sure the version of themselves they are presenting to the world is the real one — and that the standards they are applying to others are standards they themselves can meet.

Because the most successful later-life relationships tend to begin not when someone finally finds a perfect partner, but when two imperfect people decide to be honest about who they actually are and extend to each other the same fairness they have been waiting for someone to show them.

That kind of honesty changes everything. It always has.

FINAL THOUGHTS

LEAVING THE DOOR OPEN

There is something that people rarely say directly about the later seasons of life but that most of them understand from the inside. That time feels different here. Not worse - different. The days carry a weight and a clarity that earlier decades didn't have, because there is enough life behind you now to understand, in a way that wasn't possible before, that what is in front of you is not unlimited. That awareness can be quietly terrifying. It can also be, and often is, the thing that finally makes a person honest.

Honest about what they actually want. Honest about what they have been avoiding and why. Honest about whether the life they have constructed around their independence and their safety and their carefully maintained routines is the life they would choose, or simply the life they arrived at when choosing felt like too much risk.

This book has tried, throughout, to have that honest conversation. Not to judge the choices people make or to suggest that any single path through the later years is the right one. But to name what is actually happening for a great many people - the loneliness that doesn't announce itself, the expectations that eliminate everyone without quite meaning to, the fear that protection has become indistinguishable from isolation - and to hold all of it up to the light without flinching.

Because the people reading this deserve that. They have lived long enough to know the difference between a conversation that tells them what they want to hear and one that tells them something true. They have been through enough to handle honesty. What they cannot always handle, and what serves them least, is being treated as though the harder questions don't apply to them.

The harder questions do apply. They apply to everyone who has ever sat in a quiet house and felt the absence of something they couldn't quite name. Everyone who has met someone promising and found a reason to pull back before it could become something real. Everyone who has said they were fine on their own while privately wondering whether fine was enough.

To those people, the answer this book keeps returning to is not a guarantee. It is something smaller and more honest than that. It is simply this: the door can stay open. Not because opening it ensures that something will come through, but because keeping it closed ensures that nothing will.

Connection at this stage of life asks for something specific. It asks for the willingness to be seen as you actually are - not the younger version, not the uncomplicated version, not the version with the history edited out - but the real and present and fully accumulated version. It asks for patience with another person's accumulated self, because they are carrying everything their life taught them just as you are carrying everything yours did. It asks for the courage to want something and to say so, and to keep saying so even when previous chapters made that feel foolish.

That is not a small ask. But it is, for those who manage it, the thing that makes the difference between a later life that is merely comfortable and one that is genuinely full.

Some people will find the companion they are hoping for. Others will discover that their fullness comes from a different kind of arrangement - from friendship, from family, from community, from the rich interior life of a person who has learned, over many years, to be good company for themselves. Both are real. Both are worthy. What matters is not which path a person takes but whether they took it honestly - whether they chose it or simply drifted into it, whether it reflects what they actually want or what felt safest to want.

Later in life, time is the one thing that cannot be recovered. That is not a reason for despair. It is a reason for clarity. For deciding, with whatever years remain, to live as close to the truth of what you want as you can manage.

And if what you want includes someone to walk beside you - someone to share the ordinary days with, someone who understands without explanation, someone whose presence makes the quiet feel inhabited rather than empty - then the most important thing this book can say to you is also the simplest.

Keep the door open.

You don't always know what's on the other side of it until you do.

A STARTING POINT

Resources for the Journey

This book has tried to be an honest conversation rather than a prescription. What comes next belongs entirely to you. But if you are looking for places to begin or to continue, the following categories of resources are worth knowing about.

For connection and community

AARP offers an extensive network of resources for adults over fifty including local chapters, social events, and online communities where people in similar life situations connect. Their website at aarp.org is a reasonable starting point for almost any question related to life in the later years.

Local community centers, faith communities, and senior centers often host social events, classes, and group activities that create natural opportunities to meet people without the pressure of a formal dating context. Many people find that connection arrives most naturally when they are simply engaged in something they enjoy alongside other people.

Volunteering is consistently cited by older adults as one of the most effective ways to build a social network and find a sense of purpose simultaneously. Local hospitals, libraries, schools, and nonprofits welcome volunteers and the relationships that develop in those settings tend to be genuine and unhurried.

For online dating

Several platforms cater specifically to adults over fifty and a simple search for dating sites for older adults or dating apps for seniors will surface the current options. The landscape shifts regularly so rather than recommending specific platforms by name it is more useful to say this: read recent reviews from people in your age group, start with a free version before committing financially, use recent photographs, and trust your instincts when something feels off.

For deeper reading

Books on attachment styles, emotional availability, and the psychology of relationships can be valuable companions to the self-reflection this book has encouraged. A search at any library or bookstore for books on relationships, emotional intelligence, or dating later in life will surface options worth exploring. Reading widely on the subject of how people connect and why they sometimes struggle to is rarely wasted effort regardless of which specific books you choose.

For support

Therapy and counseling are worth mentioning without apology. Many people in the later years carry unprocessed grief, old relationship wounds, or patterns of behavior they have never fully examined. A good therapist is not a sign that something is wrong. It is a sign that a person takes their own inner life seriously enough to invest in understanding it. Psychology Today maintains an online therapist finder at psychologytoday.com that allows searches by location, specialty, and insurance.

If loneliness has become something more persistent and difficult, the AARP Foundation operates a free program called Connect2Affect that helps isolated older adults find connection and support.

A final note

No resource replaces the work of honest self-reflection that is the real starting point for any meaningful connection. The most useful thing anyone can do before stepping back into the search for companionship is exactly what this book has tried to encourage - to know themselves clearly, to understand what they are actually looking for and why, and to approach other people with the same patience and fairness they hope to receive.

Everything else follows from that.

ABOUT THE AUTHOR

Alice Truman writes about relationships with honesty, warmth, and a deep understanding of the emotional realities people experience throughout life. Her work focuses on the complicated spaces where love, expectations, personal history, and human vulnerability intersect. Rather than offering rigid rules or simple formulas, she approaches relationships the way many real conversations happen-thoughtfully, openly, and without pretending that life is always neat or predictable.

Much of Alice's writing explores what happens after the fairy tales fade and real life takes over. She examines how people grow, change, heal, and sometimes start over again as they move through different seasons of life. Her books encourage readers to look honestly at themselves and their relationships while recognizing that connection, understanding, and companionship often require patience, reflection, and emotional courage.

In *Is There Really Somebody for Everybody?*, Alice Truman turns her attention to one of the most common yet rarely discussed questions people face later in life: how relationships evolve as people grow older and what companionship truly means in the later years. Drawing on the experiences many people quietly share but seldom talk about openly, she explores dating, expectations, family dynamics, financial realities, and the emotional challenges of forming meaningful connections after decades of life experience.

Alice believes that relationships are not defined by perfection, but by the willingness of two people to understand each other as they are. Her writing invites readers to move beyond idealized expectations and instead embrace the honest, sometimes messy, but deeply human journey of connection.

Through her work, Alice Truman continues to encourage thoughtful conversations about love, companionship, and the ways people support one another as life unfolds.

ALSO BY ALICE TRUMAN

II'm Ready is a powerful guide for the woman who has it all together on the outside, but feels emotionally weary on the inside. Written with warmth, wisdom, and truth, this transformational book invites you to take off the emotional armor, release old patterns, and open yourself to the kind of love you truly desire - without abandoning your strength.

We Got This: In this refreshing and relatable relationship book, We Got This! serves up the essential "ingredients" that every lasting love needs. Blending wisdom, humor, and a dash of tough love, this guide is perfect for couples who want to strengthen their bond, reignite their connection, and learn how to truly serve the relationship - not just themselves.

Why Can't We Get Along?: Whether you're dating, married, or recovering from a breakup, Why Can't We Get Along? helps you understand why love feels so hard - and how to finally fix it. Packed with practical advice, emotional insight, and honest examples, this relationship guide will help you break the cycle of confusion, silence, and unmet needs.

Life's Sacred Seasons is a powerful spiritual and self-help guide that explores how to embrace each stage of life with wisdom, grace, and intention.

Made in the USA
Monee, IL
04 November 2026

67386710R00056